THE
GEORGE OPPEN
MEMORIAL
BBQ

A POEM

ERIC TYLER BENICK

the operating system digital print//document

THE GEORGE OPPEN MEMORIAL BBQ

ISBN # 978-1-946031-62-4
copyright © 2019 by Eric Tyler Benick
edited and designed by ELÆ [Lynne DeSilva-Johnson] with Anna Winham

is released under a Creative Commons CC-BY-NC-ND (Attribution, Non Commercial, No Derivatives) License: its reproduction is encouraged for those who otherwise could not afford its purchase in the case of academic, personal, and other creative usage from which no profit will accrue.

Complete rules and restrictions are available at:
http://creativecommons.org/licenses/by-nc-nd/3.0/

For additional questions regarding reproduction, quotation, or to request a pdf for review contact operator@theoperatingsystem.org

Print books from The Operating System are distributed to the trade by SPD/Small Press Distribution, with ePub and POD via Ingram, with production by Spencer Printing, in Honesdale, PA, in the USA. Digital books are available directly from the OS, direct from authors, via DIY pamplet printing, and/or POD.

This text was set in Steelworks Vintage, Europa-Light, Gill Sans, Minion, and OCR-A Standard.

Cover Art uses an image from the series "Collected Objects & the Dead Birds I Did Not Carry Home," by Heidi Reszies.

[Cover Image Description: Mixed media collage using torn pieces of paper in yellow tones, antique stamp-collecting grid-paper, and a photograph of a partial bird skeleton attached to blue-black wings laid on a sidewalk, with the book's title in vintage-styled typography overlaid.]

the operating system
www.theoperatingsystem.org
mailto: operator@theoperatingsystem.org

THE
GEORGE OPPEN
MEMORIAL
BBQ

A POEM

2019 OS SYSTEM OPERATORS

CREATIVE DIRECTOR/FOUNDER/MANAGING EDITOR: ELÆ
[Lynne DeSilva-Johnson]

DEPUTY EDITOR: Peter Milne Greiner
CONTRIBUTING EDITOR, EX-SPEC-PO: Kenning JP Garcia
CONTRIBUTING EDITOR, FIELD NOTES: Adrian Silbernagel
CONTRIBUTING EDITOR, IN CORPORE SANO: Amanda Glassman
CONTRIBUTING EDITOR, GLOSSARIUM: Ashkan Eslami Fard
CONTRIBUTING ED. GLOSSARIUM / RESOURCE COORDINATOR: Bahaar Ahsan
JOURNEYHUMAN / SYSTEMS APPRENTICE: Anna Winham
DIGITAL CHAPBOOKS / POETRY MONTH COORDINATOR: Robert Balun
TYPOGRAPHY WRANGLER / DEVELOPMENT COORDINATOR: Zoe Guttenplan
DESIGN ASSISTANTS: Lori Anderson Moseman, Orchid Tierney, Michael Flatt
SOCIAL SYSTEMS / HEALING TECH: Curtis Emery
VOLUNTEERS and/or ADVISORS: Adra Raine, Alexis Quinlan, Clarinda Mac Low, Bill Considine, Careen Shannon, Joanna C. Valente, L. Ann Wheeler, Erick Sáenz, Knar Gavin, Joe Cosmo Cogen, Charlie Stern, Audrey Gascho, Michel Bauwens, Christopher Woodrell, Liz Maxwell, Margaret Rhee, Lydia X. Y. Brown, Lauren Blodgett, Semir Chouabi, J. Lester Feder, Margaretha Haughwout, Alexandra Juhasz, Caits Meissner, Mehdi Navid, Hoa Nguyen, Margaret Randall, Benjamin Wiessner

> The Operating System is a member of the **Radical Open Access Collective**, a community of scholar-led, not-for-profit presses, journals and other open access projects. Now consisting of 40 members, we promote a progressive vision for open publishing in the humanities and social sciences.
>
> Learn more at: http://radicaloa.disruptivemedia.org.uk/about/

Your donation makes our publications, platform and programs possible! We <3 You.
http://www.theoperatingsystem.org/subscribe-join/

*We don't really know what
Reality is made of*

—George Oppen

The world is everything that is the case.

—Ludwig Wittgenstein

Here we enter
our fast
in the face of feast.

Here we lay
our bodies against
the obelisk
and form its naked cornices.

Here we throw
apples into the air
where they stick,
anti-Newtonian.

I trade flowers
for a canvas
shirt, a pocket
watch for a knife,
a loaf of bread
for samizdat.

On the spit
they are roasting
peaches. We let the hogs
mow the grass.

Somebody refers to vision
as *only a collection
of contexts.* I think
of Schopenhauer,
how he must have hated blueberries.

The boys dive
off the dock
and into the milk.

The Sicilians are drunk
on cards shouting
the one word that means
both *pick em up*
and *get fucked.*

The river blows its foghorn.
The machinists take
their cigarette breaks.
The owls are screaming
what sound like pejoratives,
but no one here speaks owl.

We run out of firewood.
I throw *The Cantos*
on the smoke. It burns
for a fortnight.

Painters make the pancakes.

A farmer and a carpenter
are trading documents. There
is commotion among the rutabagas.
Dusk begins its digging.

Here the ferry only arrives
and only one way.

Don't think I don't see you
Tawni, shucking garbanzos,
golden lovely. There is always space
in a poem for love
when it is exact.

At eight,
we stop waterboarding
bureaucrats.

At nine, daiquiris.

The Marxists arrive
with guns and plantains.

We pull a catfish
from the line.
We throw it back.
We pull a blue crab
from the line.
We throw it back.
We pull a boot
from the line.
We throw it.

My brother is in the avocado fields
kicking the rocks around.

At ten,
we start the whole thing up again.

Commandante with the Lorca hairline
is hanging apples in the abattoir
and polishing his pistol
for the high holiday.

We beat down the litigators
with their monstrous tome.
We string them from the prow
and paint their bellies
pink.

We're as
weary of war
as war is
of us.

Fred Hampton.
Fred Hampton.
Fred Hampton.

We set the caryatids free
and kerosene the pantheon.

We try to put the Catholics
in the pillory but they are too fond
of bondage.

The French are the first
to break the fast. I don't blame them.
Their wine tastes like shit
without bread.

The Germans deconstruct
a microwave
and invent a new music.

I bring fresh cotton
to the knitting party.
They crack their fingers
like turmeric.

Fela dances the fig
tree. Suffer for what?
And at whose fault?

The redwoods look
like tenements.
The leaves are going
on strike.

The white messiah
is kissing the fish again,
burying eggs in the sand,
smudging the train car.
I ask him politely
to fuck off.

Here hegemony
is a language of vegetation
not of people.
Here the tongue
is a salve.

AFTER-WORDS

A KIND OF LIMITLESS OBJECT:
ERIC TYLER BENICK IN CONVERSATION WITH LYNNE DESILVA-JOHNSON [ELÆ]

Greetings comrade! Thank you for talking to us about your process today! Can you introduce yourself, in a way that you would choose?

My name is Eric Benick. Son of Chris and Carolyn. Brother of Alex. Husband to Tawni. Native of Nashville, TN. Current resident of Clinton Hill, Brooklyn.

Why are you a poet/writer/artist?

I am not sure I know or have a creative answer to this question. All I know is, at a certain age (13-14 maybe), something clicked and I no longer had a choice.

When did you decide you were a poet/writer/artist (and/or: do you feel comfortable calling yourself a poet/writer/artist, what other titles or affiliations do you prefer/feel are more accurate)?

I don't think I ever "decided" anything. I think I found myself pulled more and more into art and then at a point nothing else made much sense or seemed a better way to spend my time. It was just a matter of survival after that. I have never felt comfortable calling myself a poet/writer/artist as those words seem to carry too much meaning for most people (myself included) and consequentially occlude or escape the labor of the art itself. I am comfortable saying that I "write poetry" or "study poetry" because the action is more present. Clarity is important to me and calling myself a poet would seem to kind of leverage or mythologize myself in way I don't think is accurate or helpful.

What's a "poet" (or "writer" or "artist") anyway? What do you see as your cultural and social role (in the literary / artistic / creative community and beyond)?

This is a pretty big ontological question that I don't feel entirely equipped to answer. I guess, in a kind of paradoxical move from the previous question, I see poets as ordinary folks gifted in some sort of elocution, abstraction, or movability. Ezra Pound is not a poet to me; he was a demagogue. Andre 3000 is a poet to me. Pieter Bruegel the Elder is a poet to me.

As far as my cultural and/or social role in the literary/artistic/creative community, I'm not sure. I think art allows possibility unlike anything else we have or have ever had access to. I think about that question a little bit more as a publisher as I am actively putting other people's work out in the world much more than my own. I think, often in long conversations with my press partner, about what work is doing, what it makes possible, who it makes more visible, how it functions as a kind of limitless object. I find that asking myself those questions about art tend to make me a more engaged individual overall and I can only hope it does the same for others.

Talk about the process or instinct to move these poems (or your work in general) as independent entities into a body of work. How and why did this happen? Have you had this intention for a while? What encouraged and/or confounded this (or a book, in general) coming together? Was it a struggle?

The George Oppen Memorial BBQ is a poem that was moved significantly by living in New York, by Oppen's own poem "Of Being Numerous," by listening to Neu! on the Metro North, by Saul Alinsky's Rules for Radicals, by interviews with Fred Hampton, by working on a farm in Italy, by Dada, by Aram Saroyan's minimalism. I have no idea why it happened. I simply found a structure that seemed to keep generating more material. Humor was also (is also) a guiding force in this poem (my poems) which made the surprise and strangeness more fun to engage in. It was surprisingly, unlike everything else, not a struggle, but that is not to also say that it was easy.

Did you envision this collection as a collection or understand your process as writing or making specifically around a theme while the poems themselves were being written / the work was being made? How or how not?

I cannot say it is a collection as it is one poem. Still, I think many of the themes alive in this poem/book are present in my other work. I don't understand anything I do while I'm doing it. I move with impulse and texture. I understand it later... if I'm lucky.

What formal structures or other constrictive practices (if any) do you use in the creation of your work? Have certain teachers or instructive environments, or readings/writings/work of other creative people informed the way you work/write?

I have no formal structures or constrictions as I am a highly anxious person and slow at generating material anyway. I sing to myself almost constantly when I am alone or with my wife impromptu jingles that I make up on the spot which I think is a cathartic, joyful way of getting a lot of shit out of my system. As far as teachers go, Aracelis Girmay is, without a doubt, the single most giving, intoxicating, ineffable, and caring poet I have ever had the privilege of working with. I strive for all of my poems to be as curious and transmutative as Aracelis.

Speaking of monikers, what does your title represent? How was it generated? Talk about the way you titled the book, and how your process of naming (individual pieces, sections, etc) influences you and/or colors your work specifically.

The title is *The George Oppen Memorial BBQ* which is an overt nod to George Oppen, poet and organizer associated with Objectivism, and the Frank Zappa composition "The Eric Dolphy Memorial Barbecue." It goes without saying I am fan of both of these artists and felt the combination of the book's humor, surrealism, direct treatment of the object, politics, and hooliganism warranted me stealing their identities/ideas for the sake of a not very clever title. Titles are profoundly important to me. Most of my work begins as a title and the title helps to guide and color the tone and shape of the poem. I have a deep love for poets who create brilliant titles. Lucie Brock-Broido, Roger Reeves, David Berman are all champions of titling.

What does this particular work represent to you as indicative of your method/creative practice? your history? your mission/intentions/hopes/plans?

The George Oppen Memorial BBQ represents to me a mission to stay alive, spirited, listening, amenable, yet spunky. As a creative practice it is very much in line with my attempts to find a parallax view to the world, to uncover objects, to maybe glimpse truth, or to make up the truth and say I glimpsed it.

What does this book DO (as much as what it says or contains)?

I think this book tries its best to be buoyant and antitotalitarian.

What would be the best possible outcome for this book? What might it do in the world, and how will its presence as an object facilitate your creative role in your community and beyond? What are your hopes for this book, and for your practice?

I think the best possible outcome for this book is that someone reads it, enjoys it, and thinks differently about something in their life. I don't spend much time thinking about best outcomes. I write what surprises and teaches me. I publish what surprises and teaches me. I can only hope my work and my practice will do the same to those who encounter it.

Let's talk a little bit about the role of poetics and creative community in social activism. I'd be curious to hear some thoughts on the challenges we face in speaking and publishing across lines of race, age, privilege, social/ cultural background, and sexuality within the community, vs. the dangers of remaining and producing in isolated "silos."

This is a smart and challenging prompt that I have nothing smart or challenging to engage it with. I think art is a communal practice. I think it requires support, empathy, friendship, patience, and love and in that way is no different than personhood. Social capital is bullshit. Singular genius isn't actually valuable. We need to make space for art just as we do people, which is no different than why we need to value labor because labor is people. Isolationism is how we effectively destroy ourselves.

Is there anything else we should have asked, or that you want to share?

No. These were all very thoughtful questions and my brain is now a mashed potato.

ABOUT THE AUTHOR

ERIC TYLER BENICK is co-founder and editor at Ursus Americanus Press, a publisher of chapbooks. His poems have appeared or are forthcoming in *The Vassar Review, Reality Beach, Bad Nudes, Graviton, decomP, Souvenir, Fruita Pulp, Fog Machine,* and elsewhere. He is a current MFA candidate for Poetry at Sarah Lawrence College. He lives in Clinton Hill, Brooklyn.

ABOUT THE COVER ART:

The Operating System 2019 chapbooks, in both digital and print, feature art from Heidi Reszies. The work is from a series entitled "Collected Objects & the Dead Birds I Did Not Carry Home," which are mixed media collages with encaustic on 8 x 8 wood panel, made in 2018.

Heidi writes: "This series explores objects/fragments of material culture--how objects occupy space, and my relationship to them or to their absence."

This chapbook also includes digital reproductions of the vintage book covers of the original *American Policy Player's Guide and Dream Book*.

ABOUT THE ARTIST:

Heidi Reszies is a poet/transdisciplinary artist living in Richmond, Virginia. Her visual art is included in the National Museum of Women in the Arts CLARA Database of Women Artists. She teaches letterpress printing at the Virginia Commonwealth University School of the Arts, and is the creator/curator of Artifact Press. Her poetry collection titled *Illusory Borders* is forthcoming from The Operating System in 2019, and now available for pre-order. Her collection titled *Of Water & Other Soft Constructions* was selected by Samiya Bashir as the winner of the Anhinga Press 2018 Robert Dana Prize for Poetry (forthcoming in 2019).

Find her at heidireszies.com

WHY PRINT:DOCUMENT?
(AND WHAT DOES THIS MEAN FOR DIGITAL MEDIA?)

The Operating System has traditionally used the language "print:document" to differentiate from the book-object as part of our mission to distinguish the act of documentation-in-book-FORM from the act of publishing as a backwards-facing replication of the book's agentive *role* as it may have appeared the last several centuries of its history. Ultimately, we approach the book as TECHNOLOGY: one of a variety of documents across a range of media that humans have invented and in turn used to archive and disseminate ideas, beliefs, stories, and other evidence of production.

Ownership and use of printing presses and access to (or restriction of) information/materials, libraries, and archives has long been a site of struggle, related in many ways to revolutionary activity and the fight for civil rights and free speech all over the world. While (in many countries) the contemporary quotidian landscape has indeed drastically shifted in its access to platforms for sharing information and in the widespread ability to "publish" digitally, even with extremely limited resources, the importance of publication on physical media has not diminished. In fact, this may be the most critical time in recent history for activist groups, artists, and others to insist upon learning, establishing, and encouraging personal and community documentation practices.

With The OS's print endeavors I wanted to open up a conversation about this: the ultimately radical, transgressive act of creating PRINT / DOCUMENTATION in the digital age. It's a question of the archive, and of history: who gets to tell the story, and what evidence of our lives, our behaviors, and/or our experiences are we leaving behind? We can know little to nothing about the future into which we're leaving an unprecedentedly digital document trail--but we can be assured that publications, government agencies, museums, schools, and other institutional powers that be will continue to leave BOTH a digital and print version of their production for the official record. Will we?

As a (rogue) anthropologist and long time academic, I can easily pull up many accounts about how lives, behaviors, experiences--how THE STORY of a time or place--was pieced together using the deep study of the archive: correspondence, notebooks, and other physical documents which are no longer the norm in many lives and practices. As we move our creative behaviors towards digital note taking, and even audio and video, what can we predict about future technology that is in any way assuring that our stories will be accurately told--or told at all? How will we leave these things for the record?

For all our years of print publication, I've said that "with these documents we say: WE WERE HERE, WE EXISTED, WE HAVE A DIFFERENT STORY", but now, with the rapid expansion of greater volume with digital and DIY printed media, we add: we ARE here, and while we are, we will not be limited in what we add value to, share, make accessible, or give voice to, by restricting it to what we can afford to print in volume.

Adding a digital series is the next chapter of *our* story: a way for us to support more creative practitioners and offer folks independent options for POD or DIY-zine-style distribution, even without our financial means changing -- which means, each book will *also* have archive-ready print manifestations. It's our way of challenging what is required to evolve and grow. Ever onward, outward, beyond.

                              Elæ [Lynne DeSilva-Johnson]. Founder& Creative Director
                                    THE OPERATING SYSTEM, Brooklyn NY 2019

THE 2019 OS CHAPBOOK SERIES

DIGITAL TITLES:

American Policy Player's Guide and Dream Book - Rachel Zolf
The George Oppen Memorial BBQ - Eric Benick
Flight Of The Mothman - Gyasi Hall
Mass Transitions - Sue Landers
Music Of Each Slain Creature - Frank Sherlock
The Grass Is Greener When The Sun Is Yellow - Sarah Rosenthal & Valerie Witte
From Being Things, To Equalities In All - Joe Milazzo
These Deals Won't Last Forever - Sasha Amari Hawkins
Ventriloquy - Bonnie Emerick
A Period Of Non-Enforcement - Lindsay Miles
Quantum Mechanics : Memoirs Of A Quark - Brad Baumgartner
Hara-Kiri On Monkey Bars - Anna Hoff

***

PRINT TITLES:

Vela. - Knar Gavin
[零] A Phantom Zero - Ryu Ando
Don't Be Scared - Magdalena Zurawski
Re: Verses - Kristina Darling & Chris Campanioni

***

PLEASE SEE OUR FULL CATALOG
FOR FULL LENGTH VOLUMES AND PREVIOUS CHAPBOOK SERIES:
HTTPS://SQUAREUP.COM/STORE/THE-OPERATING-SYSTEM/

DOC U MENT
/däkyəmənt/

First meant "instruction" or "evidence," whether written or not.

noun - a piece of written, printed, or electronic matter that provides information or evidence or that serves as an official record
verb - record (something) in written, photographic, or other form
synonyms - paper - deed - record - writing - act - instrument

[*Middle English, precept, from Old French, from Latin documentum, example, proof, from docre, to teach; see dek- in Indo-European roots.*]

Who is responsible for the manufacture of value?

Based on what supercilious ontology have we landed in a space where we vie against other creative people in vain pursuit of the fleeting credibilities of the scarcity economy, rather than freely collaborating and sharing openly with each other in ecstatic celebration of MAKING?

While we understand and acknowledge the economic pressures and fear-mongering that threatens to dominate and crush the creative impulse, we also believe that ***now more than ever we have the tools to relinquish agency via cooperative means,*** fueled by the fires of the Open Source Movement.

Looking out across the invisible vistas of that rhizomatic parallel country we can begin to see our community beyond constraints, in the place where intention meets resilient, proactive, collaborative organization.

Here is a document born of that belief, sown purely of imagination and will. When we document we assert. We print to make real, to reify our being there. When we do so with mindful intention to address our process, to open our work to others, to create beauty in words in space, to respect and acknowledge the strength of the page we now hold physical, a thing in our hand... we remind ourselves that, like Dorothy: *we had the power all along, my dears.*

THE PRINT! DOCUMENT SERIES
is a project of
the trouble with bartleby
in collaboration with
the operating system

www.ingramcontent.com/pod-product-compliance
Lightning Source LLC
Chambersburg PA
CBHW030134100526
44591CB00009B/659